Uranium

and the Lanthanides and Actinides

Nigel Saunders

www.heinemann.co.uk/library
Visit our website to find out more information about Heinemann Library books.

To order:
 Phone 44 (0) 1865 888066
 Send a fax to 44 (0) 1865 314091
 Visit the Heinemann Bookshop at www.heinemann.co.uk/library to browse our catalogue and order online.

First published in Great Britain by Heinemann Library, Halley Court, Jordan Hill, Oxford OX2 8EJ, part of Harcourt Education.
Heinemann is a registered trademark of Harcourt Education Ltd.

Editorial: Sarah Eason and Dr Carol Usher
Design: Ian Winton
Illustrations: Stefan Chabluk
Picture Research: Vashti Gwynn
Production: Edward Moore

Originated by Ambassador Litho Ltd
Printed and bound in Hong Kong, China by South China Printing Company

ISBN 0 431 16999 3
08 07 06 05 04
10 9 8 7 6 5 4 3 2 1

British Library Cataloguing in Publication Data
Saunders, N.(Nigel)
   Uranium and the lanthanides and actinides.
   - (The periodic table)
   546.4

A full catalogue record for this book is available from the British Library.

Acknowledgements
The publishers would like to thank the following for permission to reproduce photographs:
Corbis pp**4** (D Boone), **13** (Ariel Skelley), **15**, **30** (Roger Ressmeyer), **16** (Lester Lefkowitz), **19** (Jose Luis Pelacez), **23** (Mark E Gibson), **40**, **43** (Michael Boys), **45** (Yann Arthus-Bertrand), **47** (Jim Sugar Photography), **51** (Charles O'Rear), **55** (bottom), **56** (Bettmann), **57**; Getty Images p **25**; Murray Robertson p**34**; TWI Ltd. p**36**; Science Photo Library pp**10** (Roberto De Gugliemo), **21** (Maximillian Stock Ltd.), **24** (Geoff Tomkinson), **27** (Custom Medical Stock Photo), **28** (Carl Schmidt-Luchs), **31** (Wellcome Department Of Cognitive Neurology), **38**, **49** (David Ducross), **53** (NASA), **55** (top) (US Department Of Energy).

Cover photograph of uranium reproduced with permission of Corbis.

The author would like to thank Angela, Kathryn, David and Jean for all their help and support.

Every effort has been made to contact copyright holders of any material reproduced in this book. Any omissions will be rectified in subsequent printings if notice is given to the publishers.

Disclaimer
All the Internet addresses (URLs) given in this book were valid at the time of going to press. However, due to the dynamic nature of the Internet, some addresses may have changed, or sites may have ceased to exist since publication. While the author and publishers regret any inconvenience this may cause readers, no responsibility for any such changes can be accepted by either author or the publishers.

Contents

Words appearing in bold, **like this**, are explained in the Glossary

Elements and atomic structure

Everywhere you look there are different substances. Some of them are gases, such as air; others are liquids, for example water; but most of them are solids, including metals, plastics and the paper that makes this book. There are millions of different substances, but they are all made from simple components, namely **elements**.

▲
Everything in this fairground, including the rides, stalls and people, is made from some of the millions of substances in the world.

Elements and compounds

Elements are substances that cannot be broken down into anything more simple using chemical **reactions**. There are about ninety elements that occur naturally. Scientists have learned how to make over twenty more using **nuclear reactions**, including eleven of the actinides. About three-quarters of the elements are metals, such as lanthanum, the rest are non-metals, such as chlorine. Elements join together in countless different ways in chemical reactions to make **compounds**. An example of this occurs when lanthanum and chlorine react together to make lanthanum chloride. Most substances in the world are compounds, made up of two or more elements chemically joined together.

Atoms

Every substance, whether it is an element or a compound, is made up of tiny particles called **atoms**. An element is made up of just one type of atom, whereas compounds are made from two or more types of atom joined together. Individual atoms are far too tiny for us to see, even with a light microscope. If you could stack five million lanthanide atoms, which are all of a similar size, on top of each other, the pile would only be about a millimetre high!

Subatomic particles

Scientists once thought that atoms were the smallest things in the universe. They now know that atoms are made from even tinier objects called **subatomic particles. Neutrons** and **protons** are joined together in the centre of the atom to make its **nucleus**. Neutrons do not have an electrical charge, but protons are positively charged. Even smaller, negatively-charged subatomic particles, '**electrons**', are arranged around the nucleus in layers or 'shells'. This arrangement of electrons resembles the way the planets are arranged around the Sun. In fact most of an atom is empty space.

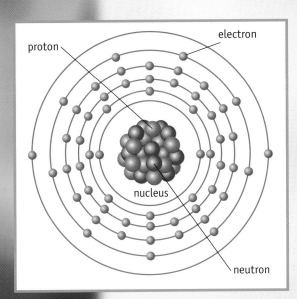

◀ This is a model of an atom of lanthanum. Each lanthanum atom contains 57 protons and 82 neutrons, with 57 electrons arranged in six shells, or energy levels, around the nucleus.

Groups

Elements react in different ways, which makes chemistry both exciting and puzzling. Several attempts were made to organize them, but Dimitri Mendeleev, a Russian chemist, was the most successful. His table, which he completed in 1869, organized similar elements into one of eight **groups**, making it far easier for chemists to predict how they might behave. Mendeleev's table was so successful that the modern **periodic table** is based upon it.

The periodic table, the lanthanides and actinides

The modern **periodic table** originates from Mendeleev's table. The **elements** are arranged in horizontal rows called **periods**, with the **atomic number** (number of **protons** in the **nucleus**) increasing from left to right. Each vertical column in the periodic table is called a **group**, and the elements in a group have similar chemical properties to each other. There are eighteen groups altogether.

The number of **electrons** an element has and how they are arranged in their shells determines the way that an element **reacts**. All the elements in a group have the same number of electrons in the shell furthest from the nucleus, called the outer shell. For example, the elements in group 2 are metals

▼ *This is the periodic table of the elements. The lanthanides and actinides are two series of similar metals and each series contains fifteen elements.*

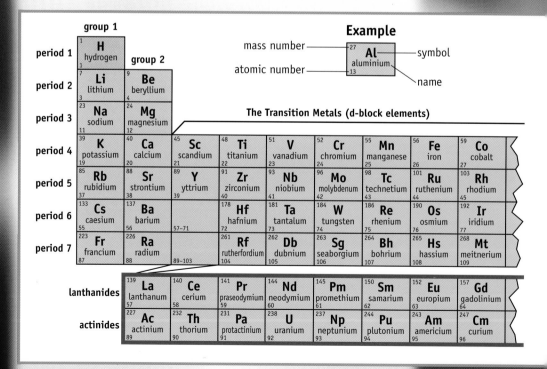

with two electrons in their outer shells, whereas those in group 7 are non-metals with seven electrons in their outer shells. The elements in both groups react quickly with other substances. The periodic table gets its name because the elements are arranged so that their chemical properties occur regularly or periodically.

The properties of the elements change gradually as you go down a group. The elements in group 0, for example, become **denser**. Balloons filled with helium (at the top of the group) rise quickly into the air, whereas balloons filled with xenon, from near the bottom of the group, fall to the ground rapidly.

The lanthanides and actinides

The 'f block' contains two periods of elements. The elements in the same period as lanthanum are called lanthanides and those in the same period as actinium are called actinides.

In this book, you will find out about the lanthanides and actinides and many of their interesting uses.

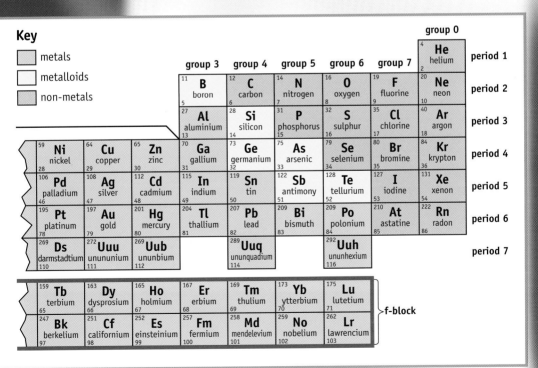

The lanthanides

All the lanthanides are shiny, silvery metals. They **react** with water and acids to produce bubbles of hydrogen gas and with oxygen in the air to produce lanthanide oxides. However, there are differences in their reactivity. For example, lanthanum and cerium become covered in a layer of white lanthanum oxide or cerium oxide quite quickly, while lutetium reacts very slowly and can stay shiny for months.

The lanthanides are all solid at room temperature, but some of them are soft enough to cut with a knife, for instance sodium and the other metals in **group** 1. The melting points of the lanthanides tend to increase across the period from lanthanum to lutetium and are all much higher than the melting points of the group 1 metals and group 2 metals, such as magnesium. The lanthanides are also much **denser** than these metals.

Lanthanides	Symbol
Lanthanum	La
Cerium	Ce
Praseodymium	Pr
Neodymium	Nd
Promethium	Pm
Samarium	Sm
Europium	Eu
Gadolinium	Gd
Terbium	Tb
Dysprosium	Dy
Holmium	Ho
Erbium	Er
Thulium	Tm
Ytterbium	Yb
Lutetium	Lu

The lanthanides are a series of fifteen elements in the periodic table, starting with lanthanum and ending with lutetium.

Not so rare

The lanthanides are often called the rare earth metals. Some really are quite rare, such as promethium, which does not seem to exist in the Earth's crust at all! It is only found in very tiny amounts in some uranium **ores**. On the other hand, cerium is more abundant in the Earth's crust than copper.

The lanthanides are used in many things including lasers, **alloys**, phosphors and glass. Most of the lanthanides are found in various **minerals** such as bastnasite, monazite and xenotime, found throughout the world. The main producer of lanthanide ores is China, but the USA, Australia and India are also major producers. A large deposit of bastnasite, discovered in California in 1949, supplies most of the lanthanides that the USA needs. Bastnasite contains a mixture of different lanthanides in **compounds** called fluorocarbonates, such as lanthanum fluorocarbonate, $LaCO_3F$. To **extract** the lanthanide metals from these minerals, they must be processed. As the lanthanides are so similar to each other this is far from easy.

▼ *This bar chart shows the quantity of each lanthanide in the Earth's crust. Copper is a widely used metal that is quite rare; on average there is only 50g of copper per tonne of Earth's crust, so you can see that in comparison most of the lanthanides are very rare indeed.*

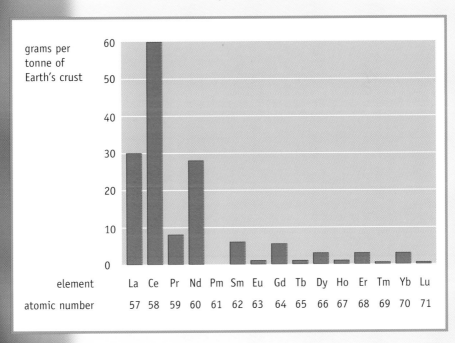

From ore to metal

It is quite difficult to separate the lanthanides from each other because they are very similar and the **minerals** in which they are found usually consist of a mixture of them. Several complex steps are needed to separate them.

This is monazite, one of the minerals that contains lanthanides. It is also the most important commercial source of thorium, an actinide. ▶

Step 1: Frothy rock

The **ore** is processed to concentrate the lanthanide minerals and remove unwanted waste materials by a process called froth flotation. The ore is crushed, then ground into a fine powder. Water and special chemicals are mixed with the powdered ore and lots of air is blown through the mixture. The unwanted rock sinks to the bottom while the lanthanide minerals float on the surface in a froth, just like a gritty milk shake!

Step 2: Acid treatment

The concentrated ore is dried and then processed to **extract** the lanthanides. It is usually treated with hydrochloric acid, which produces lanthanide chlorides, such as lanthanum chloride and lutetium chloride.

Step 3: Solvent extraction

Solvents can dissolve other substances. Water is one of many solvents and is good at dissolving substances, such as salt. Organic solvents, such as turpentine and paint thinner, contain carbon **atoms** joined to other atoms such as hydrogen and chlorine. These solvents are usually good at dissolving substances such as oil and gloss paint. The lanthanide chlorides dissolve a little in kerosene, an organic solvent, when it is mixed with some other chemicals.

Different amounts of each lanthanide chloride can dissolve in this mixture. Lutetium chloride dissolves the most, while lanthanum chloride dissolves the least and the others lie in between. The first time the lanthanide chlorides are dissolved in the kerosene mixture, the kerosene contains more lutetium chloride than lanthanum chloride. Providing the solvent-extraction step is carried out enough times, all the lanthanide chlorides can be separated from each other.

Step 4: Isolate the metals

The metals are isolated from their chlorides by heating them with a **reactive** metal such as calcium. It is possible to produce very pure metal if this step is repeated enough times, but sometimes the metals are just isolated from the concentrated ore as an **alloy** (mixture of metals).

The word equation for isolating lanthanum is:

lanthanum chloride + calcium → lanthanum + calcium chloride

This reaction happens because calcium is more reactive than lanthanum.

Lanthanum, cerium and the twins

57	La	**lanthanum**
lanthanum 139		symbol: La • atomic number: 57 • lanthanide

What does it look like? Lanthanum is a silvery metal that is soft enough to cut with a knife. It is one of the most **reactive** lanthanides, quickly reacting with oxygen in the air to form a layer of lanthanum oxide and bursting into flames when it is heated. It also reacts with water and acids.

Discovery of lanthanum

Lanthanum was discovered in 1839 by the Swedish chemist, Carl Mosander. He found the new **element** in a substance called 'ceria'. This was thirty-six years after cerium was discovered in the same substance. Mosander named lanthanum after a Greek word meaning 'overlooked'.

What are its main uses? Lanthanum is mixed with other metals to form a range of useful **alloys**, including misch metal. This is an alloy containing about 50 per cent cerium, 25 per cent lanthanum, 18 per cent neodymium and smaller amounts of other lanthanides. It is a pyrophoric alloy, which means that it gives off sparks when it is hit. Misch metal is used in cigarette lighter flints and in the manufacture of hand grenades and tracer bullets. Tracer bullets leave a trail of smoke behind them, so you can see where they go.

Nickel metal hydride batteries, called NiMH for short, are often used in laptop computers, cell phones, video cameras and cordless tools. They can be recharged quickly and are able to store twice as much energy as a nickel-cadmium 'NiCad' battery of the same size. The negative electrode in NiMH batteries is made from a nickel-lanthanum alloy, although some designs use misch metal instead of lanthanum. The negative electrode stores large amounts of hydrogen as the battery is being charged and then releases it while the battery is working.

Cracking oil

Crude oil is a mixture of different-sized **molecules** called hydrocarbons (hydrocarbons contain hydrogen and carbon **atoms** only). The small hydrocarbons are gases used for fuels, like camping gas. The really big ones are used to make black bitumen for roads. The medium-sized hydrocarbons are the most useful because they include kerosene, petrol and diesel, which are used to power aircraft, cars and lorries. Crude oil usually contains too many big molecules, but not enough of the medium-sized molecules. It has to be 'cracked' at the oil **refinery** to break down large hydrocarbons into smaller ones, such as petrol. Catalytic cracking needs **catalysts** called zeolites. Various lanthanum **compounds** are usually added to the zeolites to help stabilize them and make them more efficient.

Lanthanum glass

Lanthanum glass contains some lanthanum oxide. It is able to refract or bend light better than ordinary glass, so it is used to make high-quality lenses for telescopes and cameras. These lenses are light and produce very good images.

◀ *Cell phones, video cameras and other types of portable electronic equipment are often powered by nickel metal hydride batteries, which contain a nickel-lanthanum alloy.*

Cerium

140	
Ce	**cerium**
cerium	*symbol: Ce • atomic number: 58 • lanthanide*
58	

What does it look like?   Cerium is one of the most **reactive** lanthanides and its chemistry is slightly different from the others. It is a shiny grey metal that reacts with water and acids. It reacts with oxygen in the air to form cerium oxide and ignites when heated.

Discovery of cerium

Cerium was discovered in 1803 by the German chemist Martin Klaproth and at the same time by two Swedish chemists, Wilhlem Hisinger and Jöns Berzelius. The Swedish chemists named the new metal after Ceres, the first (and largest) asteroid to be discovered. Cerium was found in a **mineral** called ceria. It was eventually shown that ceria contained seven lanthanides in all. Pure cerium was eventually isolated by an American chemist called Alcan Hirsch in 1911.

Where is it found?   Cerium does not exist naturally as an **element**, but it is quite common in various minerals. There are about sixty grams of cerium in every tonne of rock in the Earth's crust, making it the most abundant lanthanide. This means it is about as common as lead and much more common than tin. Cerium can be **extracted** chemically rather than needing complex extraction in solvents. To produce the metal from processed lanthanide minerals, cerium chloride is heated with a more reactive metal, such as calcium. About ten thousand tonnes of cerium are produced in the world each year.

What are its main uses?   In a hot car engine nitrogen and oxygen in the air react together to form nitrogen oxides called NOx. If these escape through the exhaust pipe and into the atmosphere they dissolve in the clouds, causing acid rain. Modern car exhaust systems are fitted with catalytic converters to convert these gases into less harmful ones, such as nitrogen and carbon dioxide. Rhodium is one of the **catalysts** that reduce emissions of NOx. The catalyst works more efficiently if a little cerium is added to it.

The word equation for one of the reactions in a catalytic converter is:

nitrogen oxide + carbon monoxide → nitrogen + carbon dioxide

There are other NOx gases, too.

Polystyrene is a plastic that has a huge range of uses, including making toys, television sets and food packaging. To make each **molecule** of polystyrene, thousands of smaller styrene molecules are joined end to end. The catalyst needed to make the styrene contains cerium carbonate. This helps to keep unwanted chemicals away from the surface of the catalyst, improving its efficiency.

Carbon arc lamps are used for searchlights, movie projectors and spotlights. When electricity is passed between two electrodes made of graphite and cerium fluoride, a very powerful beam of light is produced.

◀ *These search-lights are lighting up the night sky above San Francisco in the USA. Powerful lights such as these contain electrodes made from graphite and cerium fluoride.*

Cerium oxide

Glass manufacturers use cerium oxide to improve the properties of their glass. Glass naturally has a faint green colour because small amounts of iron **compounds** are trapped in it. If cerium oxide is added during the manufacturing process, it **reacts** with the iron compounds and removes the green tint. Cerium oxide also stops harmful **ultraviolet light** from the sun passing through the glass and it is a particularly important component of aircraft windows. Exposure to ultraviolet **radiation** is greater the closer you are to the Sun.

Television sets produce small amounts of x-rays as part of their normal operation. To prevent them escaping small quantities of barium oxide and strontium oxide are added to the glass. A small amount of cerium oxide is included as well, to stop the glass gradually turning brown. Powdered cerium oxide is mixed with water to make a mixture called a slurry. This is used to polish the glass in television sets and mirrors; the surfaces of computer hard disks and computer chips. Cerium oxide is added to some plastics to stop them turning brown in sunlight.

▲ Cerium oxide can reduce the amount of harmful ultraviolet light from the sun that passes through windows into aircraft and cars. Works of art are also protected from ultraviolet light by display cases made with glass containing cerium oxide.

Lanthanides, lasers and light

'Laser' stands for Light Amplification by Stimulated Emission of Radiation. Lasers produce very intense beams of light. The lanthanides are widely used in solid-state lasers, which contain crystals.

A jump and a flash

When energy such as heat or light is supplied to an **atom**, its **electrons** can use this extra energy to jump right out of their shell and into a shell further from the **nucleus**. These excited electrons cannot stay excited for long and soon drop back to their original shell. When they do this, they give out their extra energy as a flash of light. In a laser, lots of atoms give out the same sort of light at the same time, making an intense beam of laser light.

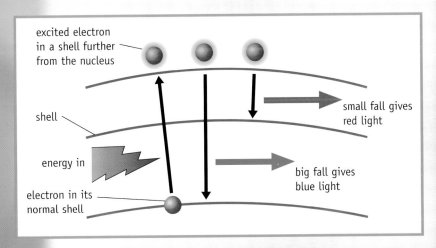

excited electron in a shell further from the nucleus

shell

energy in

electron in its normal shell

small fall gives red light

big fall gives blue light

▲
Electrons can jump into another shell if they are given the right amount of energy as heat or light. When they fall back to their normal shell, they give out this energy as light.

A rod-shaped crystal inside the laser contains the atoms that produce the laser beam. To get the laser to work, light is flashed into the crystal from the sides. This excites electrons in the crystal and they produce more light. The two flat ends of the crystal are coated with mirrors, which reflect this light back and forth inside the crystal, so that it becomes more and more intense. Eventually, a flash of laser light comes out of one end of the crystal. Various colours of laser light are produced by including different lanthanides in the crystal.

Praseodymium

141	**praseodymium**
Pr	symbol: Pr • *atomic number: 59* • lanthanide
praseodymium 59	

What does it look like?   Praseodymium is a soft, silvery metal, which **reacts** slowly with oxygen in the air, developing a green coating of praseodymium oxide. This flakes off the metal's surface, just as rust flakes off iron. To stop this happening the metal is stored under oil, like sodium in **group** 1. Praseodymium reacts with water and acids to produce hydrogen gas and green solutions of praseodymium **compounds**.

Discovery of praseodymium

In 1839, when Carl Mosander was studying the **mineral** ceria, he discovered that it contained a metal oxide with a pink colour, as well as lanthanum and cerium. Mosander called the oxide 'didymia', after the Greek word for twin because he thought it contained a new metal that was the twin of lanthanum. He called the new metal 'didymium'.

A German chemist called Carl Auer von Welsbach studied didymia more closely in 1885. He discovered that it contained two metals, not just one, as Mosander had believed. One of the metals produced green compounds, so Auer called it praseodymium after the Greek words meaning green twin. The other metal formed pink compounds and Auer named it neodymium after the Greek words for new twin.

What are its main uses?   Praseodymium compounds are used to give a yellow colour to **ceramic** tiles and glass. 'Didymium glass' contains didymia, a mixture of praseodymium oxide and neodymium oxide. Glassblowers and **welders** wear goggles made from this special glass because it filters out harmful light from their equipment that might damage their eyesight.

144	
Nd	**neodymium**
neodymium	symbol: Nd • atomic number: 60 • lanthanide
60	

What does it look like?   A soft, silvery metal, neodymium reacts with oxygen in the air to produce neodymium oxide and is therefore stored under oil. Neodymium reacts with water and acids to produce pale purple solutions of neodymium compounds and hydrogen gas.

What are its main uses?   Neodymium oxide is a sky blue **pigment** useful for colouring pottery and glass. It is added to the glass used in television sets and computer monitors because it absorbs yellow light and this helps our eyes tell red and green colours apart. Small amounts of neodymium are often added to the yttrium aluminium garnet (YAG) crystals used in lasers. These neodymium:YAG lasers produce infrared light and are used for welding metals and in medical operations. The small electric motors used in portable CD players and computer disk drives contain permanent magnets made from an **alloy** composed of neodymium, iron and boron. This alloy makes a more powerful magnet than iron alone, helping to reduce the size of the electric motor.

▲
Neodymium oxide is a blue pigment added to the glass used in television sets. It absorbs yellow light, which helps our eyes tell the red and green colours apart.

More members of the lanthanides

145 Pm promethium 61

promethium
symbol: Pm • atomic number: 61 • lanthanide

What does it look like? Promethium is very **radioactive** (see chapter six) and its **compounds** glow green in the dark. The **half-life** of its most stable **isotope**, promethium-145, is less than eighteen years, so promethium is not found naturally in the Earth's crust except in tiny quantities in some uranium **ores**. Several promethium compounds have been produced, but only in small amounts. It really is a rare earth metal!

Discovery of promethium

Jack Marinsky, Lawrence Glendenin, Harold Richter and Charles Coryell discovered promethium in 1945, in the radioactive waste from a nuclear reactor. Its name comes from the ancient Greek god Prometheus, who was punished by the gods for stealing fire from heaven.

What are its main uses? Manufacturers need to be sure that plastic film is the right thickness for its purpose, such as wrapping food and packaging goods. Some devices used to measure the thickness of plastic film contain promethium-147. Promethium-147 gives off **beta radiation**. When this **radiation** is aimed at the plastic film, the plastic stops some of it. The thicker the plastic, the less radiation gets through to the detector on the other side. Very accurate measurements of the plastic are possible, which can be as thin as 10^{-5}m (one hundredth of a millimetre).

150 Sm samarium 62

samarium
symbol: Sm • atomic number: 62 • lanthanide

What does it look like? Samarium is a silvery metal, which despite **reacting** slowly with oxygen in the air at room temperature, catches fire to produce samarium oxide when it is heated. It reacts with water and acids to produce hydrogen gas and yellow solutions of samarium compounds.

Discovery of samarium

Samarium was discovered in 1879 by a French chemist, Paul-Émile Lecoq. Its name comes from samarskite, the **mineral** in which it was found. The mineral was originally named after a Russian mine official called Samarski.

What are its main uses? Samarium oxide is added to glass so that it absorbs infrared radiation. When a neodymium laser is in use, some of the infrared laser light can escape from the sides of the crystal, which reduces its efficiency. To prevent this happening, glass containing samarium oxide is added to the side of the crystal.

The biggest use of samarium is in the production of samarium-cobalt **alloys** for making magnets. These magnets are excellent at keeping their magnetism, even at high temperatures, but neodymium-iron-boron magnets are less expensive and are now taking over. Samarium-cobalt magnets are still used in situations where resistance to high temperatures is important, such as in the aerospace industry.

This piece of metal is being cut using a laser held by a robot arm. The laser contains an yttrium aluminium garnet (YAG) crystal with small amounts of neodymium. It produces a very powerful laser beam. The glass to the side of the crystal contains samarium oxide to prevent the laser light escaping.

Europium

152	Eu	europium
	europium	symbol: Eu • atomic number: 63 • lanthanide
63		

What does it look like?   Europium, the most **reactive** lanthanide, is about as reactive as calcium in **group** 2 and reacts readily with air, water and acids. Like cerium, europium can be **extracted** chemically rather than needing complex extraction in solvents. As one of the rarer lanthanides, it is quite expensive.

Discovery of europium

Europium was discovered in some samples of impure samarium by a French chemist, Eugène Demarçay, in 1896. Demarçay named the new **element** after Europe and five years later he managed to isolate a sample of the metal.

What are its main uses?   Europium is mainly used for making phosphors. These are substances that emit light when they are exposed to **radiation**. Phosphors are very important **compounds**, without them you could not see a television picture or the image on a computer monitor.

Most television sets and computer monitors contain a type of screen called a cathode ray tube (CRT). The image in a CRT is formed when **electrons**, fired from an electron gun at the back of the CRT, hit the inside of the screen. This is coated with tiny dots containing phosphors, which glow brightly when the electrons hit them. A colour picture is made using three different phosphors, each producing red, green or blue light. The red phosphor is a mixture of europium oxide and yttrium oxide. Phosphors containing europium produce other colours too and are important for fluorescent lamps.

Fluorescent lamps

Fluorescent lamps are cheaper to run than ordinary light bulbs because they produce more light and less heat, so they are widely used in shops, factories and schools. They consist of a long glass tube with an electrode at each end.

The tube contains mercury vapour at a very low pressure. When the lamp is switched on, electrons come off the electrodes and cause some of the mercury **atoms** to become electrically charged mercury **ions**. Electricity then flows from one end of the lamp to the other through the mercury vapour. This gives some of the mercury atoms extra energy. Electrons in the atoms use this extra energy to jump out of their shells and into shells further from the nucleus. When these excited electrons drop back to their original shell, they give off light.

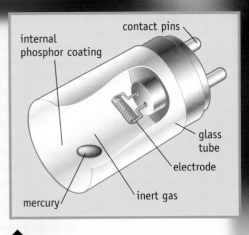

▲ Fluorescent lamps contain mercury vapour at a very low pressure, which gives off invisible ultraviolet light when electricity is passed through it. The inside of the tube is coated with chemicals called phosphors that convert the ultraviolet light into visible light.

Unfortunately, the light given off by mercury **atoms** is mostly **ultraviolet light**, which we cannot see. To convert ultraviolet light into visible light, the inside of the fluorescent tube must be coated with phosphors. A mixture of different phosphors is used, each producing a different colour. Europium oxide is usually found in phosphors that produce red or blue light. White light is produced when the different phosphors are mixed together in the right amounts.

◀ The fluorescent lamps in these aquaria contain a mixture of different phosphors that produce the desired colour of light. Europium is usually found in phosphors that produce red or blue light.

Gadolinium

| 157 **Gd** gadolinium 64 | **gadolinium** *symbol: Gd • atomic number: 64 • lanthanide* |

What does it look like? Gadolinium is a silvery metal that gradually turns dull in the air because it **reacts** with oxygen to form gadolinium oxide. This flakes off the surface of the metal, like rust flakes off iron. It also reacts with water and acids.

Discovery of gadolinium

The Swiss chemist, Jean de Marignac, discovered gadolinium in 1880. He found it in a **mineral** called gadolinite, which was named in honour of the Finnish chemist, Johan Gadolin.

What are its main uses? Gadolinium has a very high magnetic moment, which means that it is highly responsive to magnetic fields. It is very useful in technologies like magnetic resonance imaging in medicine and magneto-optical data recording in computing.

Magnetic resonance imaging, or MRI for short, allows doctors to examine the insides of their patients without opening them up. The patient lies inside a large, ring-shaped magnet and harmless radio waves are passed through them, causing some of the patient's **atoms** to give off signals. These are detected by the machine and a computer builds up an image of the patient's insides.

Compounds containing gadolinium can be injected into the patient's bloodstream first to increase the signals, so a clearer image is produced.

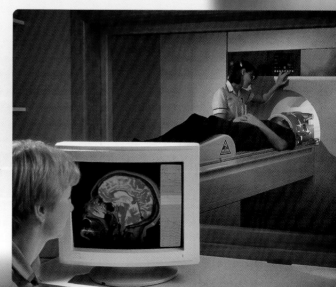

► *A magnetic resonance imaging (MRI) scanner being used to scan the brain of a patient in hospital.*

159	
Tb	
terbium	
65	

terbium

symbol: Tb • atomic number: 65 • lanthanide

What does it look like? Terbium is a silvery metal that is soft enough to cut with a knife, like sodium and potassium in **group** 1. It reacts slowly with oxygen in the air to form terbium oxide and also reacts with water and acids.

Discovery and isolation of terbium

Carl Mosander discovered terbium in gadolinite in 1843, the year after he discovered erbium. The new **element** was named terbium as the gadolinite was found near a village called Ytterby, near Stockholm.

What are its main uses? Terbium compounds are used in phosphors that produce green light. These phosphors are used in fluorescent lamps with the europium phosphors. The green colour in television pictures is provided by phosphors made from gadolinium compounds with small amounts of terbium.

Terbium-gadolinium **alloys** are used for a type of rewritable computer disk, called a magneto-optical disk. An 'MO disk' looks like an ordinary CD, but data can be recorded on it and then easily erased.

▲
This digital camcorder can record 11,000 photographs or over two hours of video on a magneto-optical disk that contains a layer of terbium-gadolinium alloy.

Dysprosium

163 **Dy** dysprosium 66	**dysprosium** *symbol: Dy • atomic number: 66 • lanthanide*

What does it look like?   Dysprosium is a silvery metal that can be cut with a knife. It **reacts** slowly with oxygen in the air to form dysprosium oxide. It also reacts with water and acids.

Discovery of dysprosium

Paul-Émile Lecoq, the French chemist who discovered samarium in 1879, discovered dysprosium seven years later. However, he was unable to isolate the metal itself, hence its name, which is from a Greek word meaning 'hard to get at'.

What are its main uses?   Dysprosium oxide is added to the special **ceramics** used to make capacitors. These are devices that can store electric charge and are widely used in electronic circuits. Nuclear reactors naturally produce high-speed **neutrons**, but some of these must be absorbed to control the **nuclear reaction**, otherwise there would be a nuclear explosion. Dysprosium oxide is one of the substances used in the control rods for some nuclear reactors because it has a high melting point and is very good at absorbing neutrons.

A type of lamp called a medium source rare earth lamp, or MSR lamp for short, contains dysprosium and holmium **compounds** mixed with other compounds. MSR lamps produce light with a good balance of colour. They are often used to light movie sets and theatre stages, so scenes look natural rather than strangely coloured.

Holmium:YAG lasers produce a beam of invisible infrared light. Surgeons use these lasers to repair damaged joints. ▶

165	
Ho	
holmium	
67	

holmium
symbol: Ho • atomic number: 67 • lanthanide

What does it look like?   Holmium will not react with oxygen in dry air, but does react slowly if the air is damp, producing holmium oxide. It reacts with water and acids and like most lanthanides is a soft, silvery metal.

Discovery of holmium
Holmium was discovered in 1878 by two Swiss chemists, Jacques-Louis Soret and Marc Delafontaine and was **extracted** a year later by Swedish chemist, Per Teodor Cleve. He named it after the Latin name for Stockholm, which is Holmia.

What are its main uses?   Holmium is used in surgical lasers called holmium:YAG lasers. These are solid-state lasers containing a crystal of yttrium aluminium garnet (the YAG in their name). Small amounts of different lanthanides can be added to YAG crystals (called doping) to produce different colours of laser light. The crystals in holmium:YAG lasers are doped with small amounts of holmium and produce short pulses of invisible infrared light, which can briefly heat up a target. Surgeons use holmium:YAG lasers to repair damaged

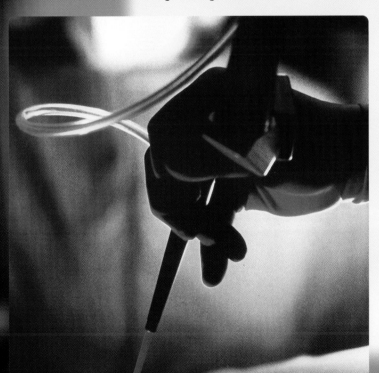

joints, such as knees, for instance, and to break up painful kidney stones. Eye surgeons use these lasers to alter the shape of the front of the eye very slightly, improving the vision of people with long sight. These people cannot focus properly on objects close to them and normally need spectacles or contact lenses.

Erbium

167		
	Er	
	erbium	
68		

erbium
symbol: Er • atomic number: 68 • lanthanide

What does it look like?   Erbium is a soft, silvery metal. It **reacts** with water and acids, but slowly with oxygen in the air.

Discovery of erbium

Erbium was discovered in gadolinite by Carl Mosander in 1842. The new **element** was named after Ytterby in Sweden, where gadolinite was found. Pure erbium was first isolated in 1934.

What are its main uses?   Vanadium is a hard metal that is often **alloyed** with steel. If it is mixed with a small amount of erbium first it becomes softer and more workable. Erbium oxide is a pleasant pink colour and is used to colour **ceramics** and glass.

Erbium is useful in amplifiers for fibre optic cables, which carry telephone and computer signals over long distances. Signals are sent as light through thin glass fibres, but as the light travels it begins to fade. If it fades too much the signal is lost, so amplifiers are needed at intervals along the cable. Erbium-doped fibre amplifiers boost the signal using laser light.

They work well because the light released by the erbium exactly matches the colour of the light used in the signal.

Erbium:YAG lasers are particularly useful for cosmetic surgery, such as smoothing skin and removing wrinkles. They produce pulses of infrared light that only go a tenth of a millimetre into the skin, removing just the outer layer.

| 169 **Tm** thulium 69 | **Thulium** symbol: Tm • atomic number: 69 • lanthanide |

What does it look like?   Thulium is a silvery metal that is soft enough to be cut with a knife, like sodium in **group** 1. It reacts with oxygen in the air to form thulium oxide and reacts easily with water and acids.

Discovery of thulium

Thulium was discovered in a sample of impure erbium oxide by the Swedish chemist, Per Teodor Cleve, in 1879. He named the new element after Thule, the Greek name for Scandinavia.

What are its main uses?   Thulium metal is very expensive. It only became available late in the 20th century and has few uses. Natural samples of thulium contain only one **isotope**, thulium-169, which is not **radioactive**. However, if it is exposed to **neutron radiation**, it is converted into radioactive thulium-170, which gives off low-energy **gamma** rays. These are similar to x-rays, so thulium-170 is used in portable 'x-ray' machines by engineers checking machines for damage, much as doctors check their patients for broken bones using x-rays.

◀ Fibre optic cables like these carry telephone and computer signals over long distances. Erbium is used in amplifiers that boost the signal as it travels along the cable.

Ytterbium

173 Yb ytterbium 70	ytterbium
	symbol: Yb • atomic number: 70 • lanthanide

What does it look like?　Ytterbium (pronounced it-ur-bee-um) is a soft, silvery metal that **reacts** with water and acids and slowly with oxygen in the air.

Discovery of ytterbium

Ytterbium was discovered in gadolinite by the Swiss chemist Jean de Marignac in 1878. It was found later by other scientists, who called it alderbarania and neoytterbia. It was finally agreed to name it ytterbium after Ytterby in Sweden, where gadolinite was found.

What are its main uses?　When heavy traffic crosses a bridge, the weight of each vehicle exerts a force on it and puts it under stress. One way to measure the stress is to use a device called a stress gauge. These are small hand-held devices that can accurately measure stresses in rocks, buildings and bridges. One type of gauge uses ytterbium to detect the stresses. Ytterbium conducts electricity, like all metals, but its resistance increases when it is pulled. This means that it becomes more difficult for electricity to flow through. If an object is put under stress, the ytterbium is pulled slightly and its resistance increases. This change in resistance can be detected using an electronic circuit, showing how much stress there is on the object.

This road has been damaged by an earthquake. You can see how far the road has been moved by the yellow lines each side of the large crack. Stress gauges containing ytterbium can measure the forces in rocks, buildings and bridges that lead to this sort of damage. ▶

175 Lu lutetium 71

lutetium
symbol: Lu • atomic number: 71 • lanthanide

What does it look like? Lutetium is pronounced 'loo-tee-shum' because it was originally spelt 'lutecium'. Lutetium is the hardest and most **dense** lanthanide. It is a silvery metal that reacts slowly with air, water and acids.

Discovery of lutetium
Lutetium was found in gadolinite, like ytterbium. Carl Auer von Welsbach, the German chemist, discovered lutetium in 1907 and called it cassiopeium. A French chemist called Georges Urbain also discovered it in the same year and named it after Lutetia Parisiorum, the Roman name for Paris.

What are its main uses? Crystals of lutetium **compounds**, containing small amounts of cerium, are used in medical imaging devices. These crystals give off a flash of light when exposed to **radiation** and are used in positron emission tomography, known as PET for short. Doctors can use PET to help them diagnose problems with the brain, such as clots and damage from strokes. The patient is injected with a harmless amount of a **radioactive** substance that gives off **subatomic particles** called positrons. These are similar to **electrons**, but have a positive electrical charge instead of a negative charge. The PET scanner detects these positrons and builds up an image of the patient's brain.

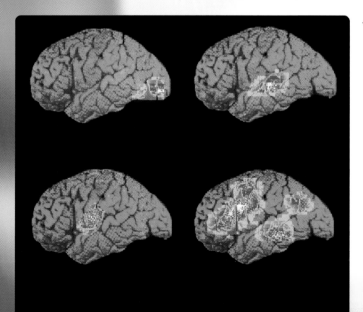

◄ Crystals containing lutetium and cerium are used in positron emission tomography (PET), which allows doctors to build up images of the brain. These PET scans show how different areas of the brain become particularly active when we see, hear or speak.

31

CHAPTER 6

The actinides and radioactivity

Four of the actinides occur naturally: actinium, thorium, protactinium and uranium. The other eleven actinides, including plutonium, are all made by **nuclear reactions.** All the actinides are silvery metals that are solid at room temperature and they are all **radioactive.** Many of them are found or made in tiny amounts and most of their uses depend on their radioactive properties. There are different forms of each actinide, called **isotopes**, which can produce different types of **radiation.**

The actinides are a series of fifteen elements in the periodic table, starting with actinium and ending with lawrencium. ▶

Actinides	Symbol
Actinium	Ac
Thorium	Th
Protactinium	Pa
Uranium	U
Neptunium	Np
Plutonium	Pu
Americium	Am
Curium	Cm
Berkelium	Bk
Californium	Cf
Einsteinium	Es
Fermium	Fm
Mendelevium	Md
Nobelium	No
Lawrencium	Lr

Isotopes

Atoms of an **element** always have the same number of **protons** in their **nucleus.** Uranium atoms, for example, always have ninety-two protons, but the number of **neutrons** can vary.

Isotopes are atoms of an element that have the same number of protons and **electrons**, but different numbers of neutrons. The most common isotope of uranium is uranium-238. The nucleus of a uranium-238 atom has 92 protons and 146 neutrons. There are several other isotopes of uranium, including uranium-235, which only has 143 neutrons. Uranium-235 behaves chemically just like uranium-238 because it still has 92 protons in its nucleus.

Half-life

The nucleus of some atoms can break up or **decay** into smaller pieces. Nobody can predict when an individual atom will decay, but if we study huge numbers of atoms we can say how long it takes for half of them to decay. The time it takes for half the atoms in an isotope to decay is called its **half-life**. This time cannot be changed by heating and cooling or by any chemical **reactions.**

Some isotopes have very unstable nuclei and they decay very quickly. The half-life of uranium-231, for example, is just over four days. Other isotopes are much more stable, for instance uranium-238, which has a half-life of around four and a half billion years.

Radiation

When a nucleus of an unstable element breaks up, it can become an isotope of a different element or another isotope of the same element. Radiation, given out when an isotope decays, can pass either through the air, our bodies, plastic or metal, depending on which type it is. **Gamma radiation** is the most penetrating type; **alpha radiation** is the least penetrating; in between is a third type of radiation called **beta radiation**.

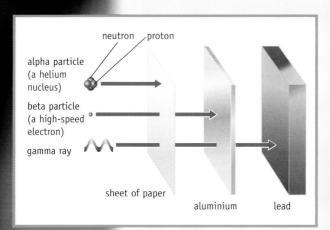

Alpha radiation is easily stopped by paper. Beta radiation can pass through paper but is stopped by sheets of aluminium. Gamma radiation will pass through paper and aluminium, but is stopped by thick sheets of lead.

Radiation hazards and health

If radiation passes into our bodies it can damage the chemicals in our cells, particularly a complex, long-chain **molecule** called deoxyribonucleic acid (DNA). DNA is the molecule that contains our genetic code. This is the code used by our cells to make the different proteins they need. If part of a DNA molecule is damaged by radiation, the code gets scrambled and may produce a protein that does not work properly. Some damaged proteins can make the cell divide uncontrollably to make many new cells, causing cancer. However, radiation used in a controlled way can help cure cancer. If a cancer cell is given a very high dose of radiation, its DNA becomes so damaged that it dies. Treating cancer using radiation is called radiotherapy.

This hazard symbol is used to warn people that the chemical inside the container is radioactive.

Actinium

89 Ac actinium 227	**actinium**
	symbol: Ac • atomic number: 89 • actinide

What does it look like?　Actinium is a soft, silvery metal that **reacts** with air and water. It is intensely **radioactive**, which is why it glows blue in the dark. It is difficult to study actinium's chemistry because it is so rare, but it seems to be very similar to lanthanum, which is immediately above it in the **periodic table**.

Discovery of actinium

The French chemist, André Debierne, discovered actinium in 1899 while helping Marie and Pierre Curie in their research. The Curies made many important discoveries involving radioactive **elements** and **radiation**. In 1898 they discovered two new elements, radium and polonium, in a uranium **ore** called pitchblende. Debierne discovered actinium in the huge amount of waste material from this research and named it after the Greek word for ray.

What are its main uses?　A tonne of pitchblende only contains about 0.1mg of actinium, but it can be made **artificially** in a nuclear reactor by exposing radium to **neutron radiation**. Actinium has not been used to make anything because it is so rare and only a few actinium **compounds** have ever been made. It is only useful for the intense radiation it produces and is mostly used for scientific research.

A sample of ▶ actinium oxide in a radiation-resistant quartz container.

Radioactive decay series

Unstable elements give off radiation and change into other elements until a stable element is formed.

Actinium-227 eventually **decays** to form lead-207, a stable **isotope** that is not radioactive. However, actinium itself comes from the decay of uranium-235. Actinium is found in tiny amounts in uranium ores such as pitchblende because some of the uranium-235 atoms have decayed. Scientists have discovered many other **nuclear reactions** like this and have pieced them together like jigsaws, to form decay series.

The actinium decay series

$$^{235}_{92}U \xrightarrow{alpha} {}^{231}_{90}Th \xrightarrow{beta} {}^{231}_{91}Pa$$

uranium   thorium   protactinium

$$^{207}_{82}Pb \xleftarrow{7\ steps} {}^{227}_{90}Th \xleftarrow{beta} {}^{227}_{89}Ac \xleftarrow{alpha}$$

lead   thorium   actinium

The other elements in the series, thorium, protactinium and uranium, are the three other naturally occurring actinides.

Chemical symbols

*The full chemical symbol for uranium-238 is $^{238}_{92}U$. The bottom number is called the **proton number** or **atomic number**, which indicates the number of **protons** in the **nucleus**. The top number is called the **mass number** and it shows the number of protons added to the number of neutrons. If you want to work out how many neutrons there are in the nucleus, you just subtract the bottom number from the top number. So the number of neutrons in an **atom** of $^{238}_{92}U$ is 238-92, which equals 146.*

Thorium

232 **Th** thorium 90	**thorium** symbol: Th • atomic number: 90 • actinide

What does it look like? Thorium is a soft, silvery metal, which **reacts** slowly with water and hydrochloric acid. It gradually becomes covered by a layer of black thorium oxide as it reacts with oxygen in the air. However, it burns with a bright white light if it is heated in air.

Discovery and extraction of thorium

Thorium was discovered in 1828 by the Swedish chemist, Jöns Berzelius, in a **mineral** called thorite (thorium silicate). He named it after Thor, the Norse god of thunder and war. Thorium is also found in other minerals such as thorianite (thorium oxide). However, monazite (one of the lanthanide minerals) is the most important commercial source of thorium. There are large deposits in Australia, India, Norway and the USA and around thirty thousand tonnes of thorium are **extracted** each year. Heating thorium oxide with a reactive metal such as calcium produces thorium metal.

What are its main uses? Thorium oxide is a solid with the highest melting point of all the oxides (nearly 3300 °C). It is widely used where resistance to high temperatures is important, for example in laboratory crucibles. Tungsten-thorium **alloys**, containing two per cent thorium oxide, are used in tungsten inert gas **welding** or TIG for short.

▶ Electrodes made from tungsten-thorium alloys are used in tungsten inert gas welding, shown here.

In TIG, heat is generated by making electricity arc or jump between two tungsten-thorium alloy electrodes. The small amount of thorium in the electrodes makes them harder and it is easier to start the electric arc. Magnesium-thorium alloys that contain three per cent thorium are used to make the skin panels and nose cones of missiles.

Thorium oxide is used in gas mantles for camping lanterns. Carl Auer Von Welsbach, the German chemist who discovered neodymium, praseodymium and lutetium, invented the Welsbach gas mantle in 1885. He soaked cotton in solutions of lanthanum nitrate, cerium nitrate or thorium nitrate, left them to dry and then burned them. Welsbach found the remains formed a mesh of metal oxide, which when heated in a flame, emitted bright, white light. He discovered that thorium oxide with one per cent cerium oxide made the best mantles. Welsbach gas mantles were widely used for lighting streets and homes until the middle of the twentieth century, when gas lighting was eventually replaced by electric lighting.

Since Marie Curie showed that thorium is **radioactive** in 1898 it has mostly been replaced by other metals, especially the lanthanides, but it is used as a component of some nuclear fuels.

The thorium decay series

Thorium **decays** eventually to form stable lead-208, which is not radioactive. There is a thorium decay series, which is slightly different to the actinium decay series, although actinium is still produced. Radium, a **group** 2 **element** discovered by Marie Curie in 1898, is also formed.

The thorium decay series

$$^{232}_{90}\text{Th} \xrightarrow{\ alpha\ } {}^{228}_{88}\text{Ra} \xrightarrow{\ beta\ } {}^{228}_{89}\text{Ac}$$

thorium   radium   actinium

$$^{208}_{82}\text{Pb} \xleftarrow{\ 6\ steps\ } {}^{224}_{88}\text{Ra} \xleftarrow{\ alpha\ } {}^{228}_{90}\text{Th} \xleftarrow{\ beta\ }$$

lead   radium   thorium

Protactinium

231 Pa	protactinium
91 protactinium	symbol: Pa • atomic number: 91 • actinide

What does it look like? Protactinium is the third rarest natural **element**, which makes it very expensive. It is very **radioactive** and needs to be handled with great care. Very little is known about protactinium's other chemical properties. It has no uses apart from scientific research.

Discovery of protactinium

When Dimitri Mendeleev worked out his **periodic table** in the late 19th century, he left some gaps for elements he believed were yet to be discovered. He left one gap between thorium (**proton number** 90) and uranium (proton number 92). With the help of the periodic table, chemists predicted the properties of the missing element, which made it easier to search for. In 1913, Kasimir Fajans and Otto Göhring managed to find an **isotope** of the missing element while studying the uranium **decay** series. They had discovered protactinium-234. They called it brevium because it has such a brief half-life – just over six hours!

In 1917, two groups of scientists discovered another protactinium isotope in pitchblende. One of the groups, Otto Hahn and Lise Meitner, suggested the name protoactinium because the element decayed to form actinium. The name was shortened to protactinium in 1949. In 1927, Aristid Grosse isolated a tiny amount of white protactinium oxide in the USA. Seven years later he managed to produce some pure protactinium by converting the oxide into protactinium iodide. When he heated this it broke down to form protactinium and iodine.

The uranium decay series
Protactinium was discovered while scientists were investigating the **decay** series of uranium. The most abundant or common natural uranium isotope, uranium-238, slowly decays to form thorium-234. This gives off **beta radiation** and becomes protactinium-234, which in turn eventually decays to form lead-206. This is a stable isotope and not radioactive.

The uranium decay series

$$^{238}_{92}U \xrightarrow{\text{alpha}} {}^{234}_{90}Th \xrightarrow{\text{beta}} {}^{234}_{91}Pa \xrightarrow{\text{beta}} {}^{234}_{92}U$$

uranium   thorium   protactinium   uranium

$$^{206}_{82}Pb \xleftarrow{\text{9 steps}} {}^{226}_{88}Ra \xleftarrow{\text{alpha}} {}^{230}_{90}Th \xleftarrow{\text{alpha}}$$

lead   radium   thorium

*Protactinium comes from uranium, which is why it is found in uranium **ores**.*

The four naturally occurring actinides
The four naturally occurring actinides are closely related through the various radioactive decay series. This explains why actinium, thorium and protactinium are found in uranium ores and why some are rare while others are not. Uranium is the last naturally occurring element. It is relatively abundant and has many uses.

Otto Hahn (1879–1968) and Lise Meitner (1878–1968) (opposite) discovered an isotope of protactinium in 1917. They named the new element protoactinium, which was shortened to protactinium in 1949.

Uranium

238	U	uranium
92	uranium	symbol: U • atomic number: 92 • actinide

uranium
symbol: U • atomic number: 92 • actinide

What does it look like?

Uranium is a silvery metal that is nearly as **dense** as gold. Although it **reacts** with acids, it reacts slowly with oxygen in the air unless it is powdered, then it bursts into flames. It is **radioactive** and produces **alpha radiation**.

*This is a disc of uranium metal. Notice the gloves the person holding it is wearing. These protect them from the **radiation** uranium emits.*

Discovery of uranium

Martin Klaproth, a German chemist, discovered uranium in 1789. He found it in the **mineral** pitchblende, which contains uranium dioxide. Klaproth named the new **element** after the planet Uranus, which had been discovered by William Herschel eight years earlier. Eugène Péligot, from France, was the first chemist to isolate uranium metal in 1841 by heating uranium tetrachloride with potassium.

Where is it found?

Uranium is not found as a pure metal, but it is fairly abundant in various minerals. On average, there are about two grams of uranium in every tonne of rock in the Earth's crust, making it about as common as tin, and more plentiful than gold or silver. The most important uranium **ore** is pitchblende, also called uraninite. The largest deposits of uranium ore are found in Australia, Kazakhstan and Canada. About forty thousand tonnes of uranium are produced in the world each year, mostly in Canada.

Yellow cake

Several complex steps are needed to **extract** uranium from its ore. The ores are processed to produce the solid sodium diuranate, $Na_2U_2O_7$, which is called 'yellow cake'. This is the form in which uranium is usually bought and sold.

Isolating uranium metal

Uranium metal is isolated from yellow cake in two main steps. The yellow cake is first processed to produce uranium dioxide, UO_2. This is heated with hydrogen fluoride to produce uranium tetrafluoride, UF_4.

*The word equation for a step in uranium ore **refining** is:*

$$\text{uranium dioxide} + \text{hydrogen fluoride} \rightarrow \text{uranium tetrafluoride} + \text{water}$$

*This is a reaction between a **base** (uranium dioxide) and an acid (hydrogen fluoride) to produce a salt and water.*

Uranium metal is produced from uranium tetrafluoride using the Ames process, which is similar to Péligot's original method. The uranium tetrafluoride is heated to over 1000 °C with a reactive metal such as magnesium, producing uranium metal and waste containing magnesium fluoride.

The word equation for the Ames Process is:

uranium tetrafluoride + magnesium → uranium + magnesium fluoride

*This reaction happens because magnesium is more reactive than uranium and is able to displace uranium from its **compounds**.*

Uranium and the discovery of radioactivity

Henri Becquerel discovered radioactivity by accident in 1896. He left photographic plates next to uranium ore in the dark. When he developed them they were foggy. The radiation from the uranium had caused the chemicals in the photographic plate to break down, just as they do when light hits them.

Uses of uranium

Uranium is used as a fuel by nuclear power stations and in the manufacture of nuclear weapons. Natural uranium is a mixture of different uranium **isotopes**, although less than one per cent is uranium-235. However, nuclear power stations need enriched uranium containing three per cent to five per cent uranium-235 and atomic weapons require highly enriched uranium containing over ninety per cent uranium-235. Natural uranium has to be processed to increase the amount of uranium-235. The left-over material is called depleted uranium because it contains a third of the uranium-235 found in natural uranium. Depleted uranium is less **radioactive** than natural uranium because it contains less uranium-235.

Depleted uranium

Uranium is a hard and very **dense** metal, almost as dense as gold or tungsten. Depleted uranium is therefore useful for making objects that need to be small and heavy, like the armour-piercing shells used by the military to destroy tanks. It is also made into sinker bars, which are used by the oil industry to sink scientific instruments to the bottom of oil wells.

In the past, depleted uranium was used in aircraft as a counterweight to maintain the centre of gravity. Jumbo jets built in the 1960s each contained around 350kg of depleted uranium in their tail sections. This has now been replaced by tungsten because of the dangers of **radiation**. Depleted uranium is also used to prepare uranium **compounds** for other uses.

Electron microscopy

The **electron** microscope allows biologists to study objects that are too small to be seen with an ordinary light microscope. They add a drop of uranium ethanoate (usually known as uranyl acetate) solution to 'stain' their samples. This helps to give a good image in the microscope because uranium is very dense and scatters electrons really well.

Glazes and glass

Uranium compounds are coloured and make good **pigments**. Although they were used in glass and pottery glazes for many years, modern glass and glazes do not contain uranium compounds because of the radiation they produce. 'Vaseline glass' is a type of antique glass that was widely used to produce ornamental objects. It contains uranium(VI) oxide and has an attractive greenish-yellow appearance. Glass containing a small amount of uranium(IV) oxide is yellow with a green tint, while uranium(V) oxide makes glass with a black tint. Pottery glazes containing sodium diuranate, $Na_2U_2O_7$, are yellow, while uranium oxide, U_3O_8, produces an olive green glaze. Glazes containing uranium(IV) oxide are bright red-yellow.

▲ These attractive pieces of glassware are made from greenish-yellow Vaseline glass, which is a type of antique glass that contains uranium(VI) oxide.

Roman numbers

Chemists use Roman numbers to tell the different uranium oxides apart. Uranium dioxide, UO_2 is uranium(IV) oxide, pronounced 'uranium four oxide'. Uranium(V) oxide (uranium five oxide) is U_2O_5 and UO_3 is uranium(VI) oxide (uranium six oxide).

The most important uses of uranium, however, involve harnessing its nuclear properties.

Bombs and reactors

When an **atom** is split the process is called fission; heat and **radiation** are produced. This may happen suddenly if the **nucleus** is unstable, when it is called spontaneous fission. Some atoms can be forced to split by firing **neutrons** at them. This is called induced fission and is the process behind atomic bomb and nuclear reactor technology.

Chain reactions

Uranium-235 is particularly easy to split by induced fission. When a neutron hits the nucleus of a uranium-235 atom, the nucleus becomes unstable and splits into two smaller ones. Heat and **gamma radiation** are released and two more neutrons are shot out. These neutrons may go on to split more uranium-235 atoms. This is called a chain reaction.

Critical mass

In a piece of uranium where induced fission is happening, some of the neutrons escape without splitting other uranium atoms. If the piece of uranium is too small, most of the neutrons escape and the chain reaction eventually stops. If there is the right amount of uranium, called the **critical mass**, the chain reaction carries on at a steady rate (on average each uranium atom split causes one more atom to split). However, if there is too much uranium, called a supercritical mass, something else happens.

Atomic bombs

In a supercritical mass, each uranium atom split causes more than one other atom to split, causing a runaway **nuclear reaction**. So much energy is released in a short time that a nuclear explosion happens. A typical bomb contains a supercritical mass of uranium, but in separate pieces to stop the nuclear reaction starting. When these pieces are slammed together to make a single ball, the bomb detonates. The first atomic bomb used in a war was a uranium bomb called 'Little Boy', which exploded over the Japanese city of Hiroshima on 6 August 1945. About 66,000 people were killed and 69,000 were injured directly. Many people died from cancer long after the bombing.

Nuclear reactors

The first nuclear reactor was built by a team led by Enrico Fermi at the University of Chicago and was started up on 2 December 1942. The reaction in a nuclear reactor is controlled so that it is critical or just slightly supercritical. This is achieved by using boron control rods. These absorb neutrons and stop them splitting uranium atoms. The heat produced by the nuclear reaction is used to make steam. This drives turbines that turn electricity generators, just like a conventional coal-fired power station. Nuclear power stations provide factories and millions of homes with electricity.

◀ *This is a nuclear reactor core viewed from above. In the middle of the photograph you can see a used fuel rod being removed from the reactor under water.*

When things go wrong

Nuclear power stations are designed to be very safe because if things go wrong the consequences are disastrous. In 1979, at a nuclear power station on Three Mile Island in Pennsylvania, USA, part of the reactor core was not cooled properly. The reactor was contaminated and small amounts of **radioactive** substances escaped, but there were no immediate deaths or injuries. Seven years later, a nuclear reactor exploded near Chernobyl in the Ukraine. It was not a nuclear explosion, but huge amounts of radioactive substances still escaped into the atmosphere and were spread by the winds and air currents throughout Europe and beyond. Local people still suffer from illnesses because of their exposure to radiation.

The artificial actinides

Uranium **atoms** are the heaviest natural atoms, with ninety-two **protons** in the **nucleus**. Atoms with more protons, called transuranium **elements**, have to be made **artificially** by converting one element into another. You cannot do this using a chemical **reaction**, which is why the ancient alchemists failed to 'get rich quick' while trying to convert lead into gold. The only way you can convert one element into another is by a **nuclear reaction**. Whenever a nuclear bomb explodes, some transuranium elements are made. Einsteinium and fermium were discovered in the fallout from the first hydrogen bomb.

What's in a bomb?

There are two basic types of nuclear reaction and both produce **radiation** and lots of energy. Fission reactions happen when the nuclei of large atoms, such as uranium and plutonium, break apart. Fusion reactions occur when the nuclei of small atoms, such as hydrogen atoms, join together to make larger nuclei. Atomic bombs use fission reactions and hydrogen bombs use fusion reactions.

The nuclear reactions in nuclear reactors also make some transuranium elements. Americium, the fourth transuranium element discovered, was found in the waste from a nuclear reactor. The rest of the artificial actinides were made by smashing high-speed particles into metal targets, using a machine called a cyclotron.

The cyclotron is a type of particle accelerator invented by Ernest Lawrence. A particle accelerator makes particles move faster and faster. In a cyclotron, the particles are shot round and round in a spiral. The first cyclotron was built in 1931 and was only about 10cm in diameter. Modern cyclotrons can be many metres in diameter and accelerate particles to about 75 per cent of the speed of light. If you could hitch a ride on one of those particles, you could get to the Sun in eleven minutes! For a cyclotron to work the particles must have an electrical charge. They are usually positively charged **ions** (atoms with **electrons** removed).

This scientist is working on a small cyclotron, a type of particle accelerator that whirls **subatomic particles** around at high speeds.

237 **Np** neptunium 93	**neptunium** symbol: Np • atomic number: 93 • actinide

What does it look like? Neptunium was the first transuranium element to be discovered. It is a silvery metal, a solid at room temperature and like all the other transuranium elements, **radioactive**. It reacts with oxygen to form brown neptunium oxide and reacts with water and acids. Solutions of neptunium **compounds** have a violet colour.

Discovery of neptunium

In 1940 Edwin McMillan and Philip Abelson bombarded some uranium-238 with **neutrons** at the Lawrence Berkeley National Laboratory in California and made a new element. The new element was called neptunium because it is the next element after uranium in the **periodic table** and Neptune is the next planet from the Sun after Uranus. Neptunium is made in nuclear reactors as part of their normal operation and is now **extracted** from nuclear wastes. However, it has little practical use apart from scientific research.

Plutonium

<table>
<tr><td>244
Pu
plutonium
94</td><td>**plutonium**
symbol: Pu • atomic number: 94 • actinide</td></tr>
</table>

What does it look like? Plutonium is solid at room temperature. It is a silvery metal that **reacts** with oxygen in the air, forming a layer of plutonium oxide on its surface that gives it a faint yellow colour. Plutonium feels warm because the **alpha radiation** it produces releases energy. It reacts with water and acids.

Discovery of plutonium

Plutonium was discovered by Glenn Seaborg, Edwin McMillan, Joseph Kennedy and Arthur Wahl in 1940. They used a cyclotron at the Lawrence Berkeley National Laboratory to bombard uranium **atoms** with deuterons. These are **ions** of a hydrogen **isotope** and consist of a **proton** and **neutron** stuck together. Plutonium was the second transuranium **element** discovered and it was named after Pluto, the next planet from the Sun after Neptune.

What are its main uses? All nuclear reactors produce plutonium-239 from uranium-238 as part of their normal operation. The spent fuel is processed to **extract** the plutonium-239, which is then used as a fuel itself in a type of nuclear reactor called a fast-breeder reactor. Plutonium-239 is also used in nuclear weapons because its **critical mass** is about a fifth of the critical mass of uranium-235. This means that weapon designers can produce smaller bombs or more powerful bombs of a similar size.

The second and last nuclear bomb used in World War Two was a plutonium bomb called 'Fat Man'. It was dropped on Nagasaki, a Japanese city, on 9 August 1945. This bomb killed about 39,000 people and injured 25,000, not including the extra deaths caused by cancer long after the bombing.

Radioisotope thermoelectric generators

Plutonium-238 is used in radioisotope thermoelectric generators. These are called RTGs for short and are nuclear batteries. In an RTG, heat is produced by the **radioactive decay** of plutonium-238, which warms a device called a thermocouple. This consists of two different metals joined together and produces electricity when heated.

RTGs are very reliable because they have no moving parts and their small size makes them ideal for powering space probes. The RTGs in modern probes are all powered by plutonium-238, as its **half-life** is nearly eighty-eight years, allowing space probes to remain working in space for a long time. Other radioactive **isotopes** such as polonium-210 have been tried, but their half-lives are shorter and cause probes to run out of power too quickly.

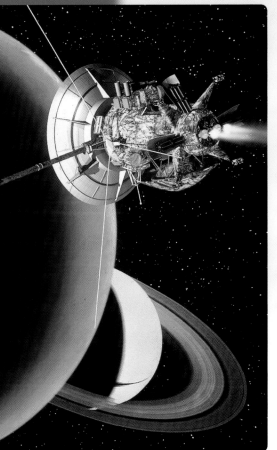

The Cassini-Huygens space probe, launched in October 1997, is designed to reach Saturn after a seven-year journey. Electricity for the probe is generated using three RTGs (radioisotope thermoelectric generators) that contain plutonium-238.

Not in my backyard!

The plutonium-239 produced in nuclear reactors has a very long half-life of 24,110 years. The disposal of this radioactive material is an enormous problem. It cannot be left in the reactor or dumped into an ordinary waste tip and must be prevented from falling into the hands of terrorists, who might use it to make a bomb. Many countries are trying to find places where they can bury it deep underground, but scientists have to predict whether it will still be safe in the future, which is a hard thing to do. Not surprisingly, nobody wants to live near a nuclear store.

Americium

243 **Am** americium 95	**americium** *symbol: Am • atomic number: 95 • actinide*

What does it look like? Americium is a **dense**, silvery metal, which is solid at room temperature, but easily shaped. Americium **reacts** with oxygen in the air to make americium oxide and also reacts with water and acids. Several americium **compounds** have been made, including brown americium oxide and pink americium chloride. Americium needs careful handling because it gives off **alpha** and **gamma radiation**.

Discovery of americium

Americium was the fourth transuranium **element** to be discovered. Glenn Seaborg, Ralph James, Leon Morgan and Albert Ghiorso, working at the University of Chicago in 1944, found it in a sample of plutonium from a nuclear reactor. The new element was named after America where it was found.

▶ *Americium is used in smoke detectors. When there are house fires like this one, smoke detectors save lives by giving an early warning so the inhabitants can escape in time.*

What are its main uses? The uses of americium rely on the **radiation** it produces. Engineers find its gamma rays useful for checking machines for cracks and other damage, rather as doctors use x-rays to check for broken bones in their patients. Glass manufacturers need to be able to check the thickness of the glass as it is being made. Americium produces alpha radiation. The thicker the glass, the less radiation goes through it. It is possible to work out the thickness of the glass by measuring the amount of radiation getting through. Another very important use of americium is in smoke detectors, which means you probably have some americium in your home.

Smoke detectors

Smoke detectors are small devices that sound an alarm if there is a fire. They are quite cheap and save lives by giving an early warning. One type, called a photoelectric detector, is activated when smoke from a fire blocks a beam of light.

The other type, called an ionization detector, contains a tiny amount of americium-241. The radioactive americium is safely sealed inside a small aluminium cylinder called an ionization chamber.

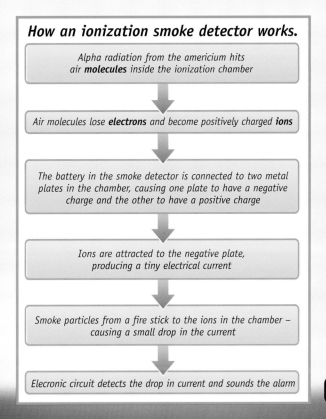

How an ionization smoke detector works.

*Alpha radiation from the americium hits air **molecules** inside the ionization chamber*

*Air molecules lose **electrons** and become positively charged **ions***

The battery in the smoke detector is connected to two metal plates in the chamber, causing one plate to have a negative charge and the other to have a positive charge

Ions are attracted to the negative plate, producing a tiny electrical current

Smoke particles from a fire stick to the ions in the chamber – causing a small drop in the current

Elecronic circuit detects the drop in current and sounds the alarm

Curium

247
Cm
curium
96

curium

symbol: Cm • atomic number: 96 • actinide

What does it look like? Curium is a silvery metal that is solid at room temperature and has a **density** similar to that of mercury. This means that even small pieces are heavy. Curium **reacts** with water, acids and oxygen in the air to form curium oxide. Several **compounds** of curium have been made, including curium chloride, $CmCl_3$, a yellow compound also called curious chloride.

Discovery of curium

Curium, the third transuranium **element**, was discovered in 1944. Helium **ions** were fired into some plutonium, using the cyclotron at the Lawrence Berkeley National Laboratory, California. When Glenn Seaborg, Albert Ghiorso and Ralph James studied this plutonium later at the University of Chicago they discovered traces of a new element.

Curium was named after Marie and Pierre Curie, who discovered polonium and radium at the start of the twentieth century. It is now made in several steps, which involve bombarding plutonium with **neutrons**. Isadore Perlman and Louis Werner first isolated pure curium metal in 1951 by reacting curium fluoride with barium metal vapour.

What are its main uses? Curium is very **radioactive** and gives off **alpha radiation**. So much heat is generated that solutions of curium compounds may eventually boil on their own. Scientists have investigated whether curium could be used as an alternative to plutonium in the radioisotope thermoelectric generators used in space probes because of this. Unfortunately, curium also gives off powerful **gamma radiation** and extra shielding would be needed to protect the people building the probe.

Curium has another important use in space probes. Both Vega (launched by the Russians to Venus in 1984) and Pathfinder (sent to Mars by the Americans in 1996) contained a device called alpha proton x-ray spectrometer, which measures the amount of every element in rock, except hydrogen. Curium-244 provides the alpha radiation this instrument needs to work.

▲

*A probe called Pathfinder landed on Mars in 1997 and released a robotic vehicle called Sojourner. This photograph shows Sojourner analysing a rock with a device that uses the **radiation** from curium.*

247 **Bk** berkelium 97	**berkelium** *symbol: Bk • atomic number: 97 • actinide*

Glenn Seaborg, Stanley Thompson and Albert Ghiorso first made berkelium in 1949. Working at the Lawrence Berkeley National Laboratory, they used a cyclotron to fire helium ions at an americium target. The scientists named the new element berkelium after Berkeley, in California, where the laboratory is based.

The element is now made by bombarding curium with neutrons. Several berkelium compounds have been made, including berkelium fluoride, which dissolves in water to form a green solution. At the moment berkelium has no uses apart from scientific research. Berkelium-247 has a **half-life** of over a thousand years and slowly **decays** to form americium again.

Californium

251 **Cf** californium 98	**californium** *symbol: Cf • atomic number: 98 • actinide*

Discovery of Californium

Californium was first made at the Lawrence Berkeley National Laboratory in California in 1950. Stanley Thompson, Kenneth Street, Albert Ghiorso and Glenn Seaborg used a cyclotron to fire helium **ions** at a target containing curium. They named the new **element** after California.

Californium atoms are now made by bombarding plutonium with **neutrons** in several stages. Although metallic californium has not been isolated, several of its **compounds** have been made. These include californium chloride, $CfCl_3$, which dissolves in water to make a green solution. The most stable **isotope** is californium-251, which has a **half-life** of around nine hundred years, and breaks down to form curium. However, californium-252 is a very powerful source of neutrons, and is used in 'neutron activation analysis'. This is a method of detecting small amounts of various elements in **minerals** such as coal.

252 **Es** einsteinium 99	**einsteinium** *symbol: Es • atomic number: 99 • actinide*

The world's first hydrogen bomb was detonated at Eniwetok atoll in the Pacific Ocean on 1 November 1952. It was code-named 'Mike', from the radio call sign for 'M', the first letter of 'megatonne'. The explosion produced a lot of **radioactive** fallout, which scientists were keen to analyse for new elements made in the explosion. Gregory Choppin, Bernard Harvey, Stanley Thompson and Albert Ghiorso, working at the Lawrence Berkeley National Laboratory, discovered einsteinium in the fallout. At first, their discovery was kept a secret because of its connection with the hydrogen bomb.

The new element was
named after Albert
Einstein, the physicist
famous for his theories
on relativity. Einsteinium
is now made in several stages by firing high-speed neutrons
at plutonium. Little is known about its chemistry and it is
only used in research. The most stable isotope, einsteinium-
252, **decays** to form fermium, californium and berkelium.

257 **Fm** fermium 100	**fermium** symbol: Fm • atomic number: 100 • actinide

Fermium was also discovered in 1952 in the fallout from the
first hydrogen bomb's explosion by the same team who
discovered einsteinium, although they kept its discovery
secret for a while too. It was named in honour of Enrico
Fermi, who was responsible for building the first nuclear
reactor at the University of Chicago in 1942. Fermium is now
made in several stages by bombarding plutonium with high-
speed neutrons. Fermium-257, its most
stable isotope, has a half-life of a
hundred days and breaks down to form
californium. Some of fermium's
chemistry is known, but it has no uses
except for research.

Element number 100 is named after
Enrico Fermi (1901–1954), seen here.
Fermi was born in Italy but emigrated to
the USA in 1938. His team built the
world's first nuclear reactor in a make-
shift laboratory under the stadium at the
University of Chicago in 1942.

Mendelevium

258 **Md** mendelevium 101	**mendelevium** *symbol: Md • atomic number: 101 • actinide*

Mendelevium was first made in 1955 by Gregory Choppin, Bernard Harvey, Stanley Thompson, Albert Ghiorso and Glenn Seaborg at the Lawrence Berkeley National Laboratory. They fired helium **ions** at einsteinium using a cyclotron and produced a few **atoms** of a new **element**. The scientists named it in honour of Dimitri Mendeleev who produced the first **periodic table**. Mendelevium is only used in research and little is known about its chemistry. The most stable **isotope**, mendelevium-258, has a **half-life** of 51 days and **decays** to form einsteinium again.

This is Dimitri Mendeleev (1834–1907), the Russian chemist who developed the periodic table of elements. Mendelevium, element number 101, was named in his honour after its discovery in 1955.

259 **No** nobelium 102	**nobelium** *symbol: No • atomic number: 102 • actinide*

In 1957, a group of scientists working at the Nobel Institute of Physics in Sweden thought they had made this element. They named it after Alfred Nobel. He was the man who invented dynamite and left a legacy in his will to found the Nobel Prizes. Firing helium ions, which are relatively small particles, at metal targets, had made other transuranium elements. However, nobelium atoms are too big to be made this way, so scientists used a cyclotron to bombard curium with carbon ions. Unfortunately, it eventually turned out that they were mistaken and they had not made the new element after all.

Nobelium was reliably made for the first time in 1958 by Albert Ghiorso, Torbjorn Sikkeland, John Walton and Glenn Seaborg working at the Lawrence Berkeley National Laboratory. They had the right to name the new element themselves because they were the discoverers, but decided to keep its name. Nobelium has no uses apart from scientific research. Its most stable isotope is nobelium-259, which has a half-life of only 58 minutes and breaks down to form mendelevium and fermium.

| 262 **Lr** lawrencium 103 | **lawrencium** *symbol: Lr • atomic number: 103 • actinide* |

Lawrencium was first made in 1961 at the Lawrence Berkeley National Laboratory in California by Albert Ghiorso, Torbjorn Sikkeland, Almon Larsh and Robert Latimer. They made several isotopes of the new element by firing boron ions at high speed into a few micrograms of californium. Lawrencium was named after Ernest Lawrence, the inventor of the cyclotron. This was the machine that made the discovery of the other transuranium actinides possible, and the Lawrence Berkeley National Laboratory itself is named in his honour.

The original chemical symbol for lawrencium was Lw, but it was changed to Lr in 1965. Lawrencium has no uses outside scientific research. Its most stable isotope is lawrencium-262 that has a half-life of just 3.6 hours, decaying to form nobelium.

◀ This is Ernest Lawrence (1901–1958), standing on a hillside overlooking the Lawrence Berkeley National Laboratory at the University of California in the USA. Lawrence invented the cyclotron in 1929 and lawrencium, element number 103, is named after him.

Find out more about the 'f block' metals

The table below contains some information about the properties of the lanthanides.

Element	Symbol	Atomic number	Melting point (°C)	Boiling point (°C)	Density (g/cm³)
Lanthanum	La	57	921	3457	6.1
Cerium	Ce	58	798	3426	6.8
Praseodymium	Pr	59	931	3512	6.6
Neodymium	Nd	60	1021	3068	7.0
Promethium	Pm	61	1168	2727	7.2
Samarium	Sm	62	1077	1791	7.5
Europium	Eu	63	822	1597	5.2
Gadolinium	Gd	64	1313	3266	7.9
Terbium	Tb	65	1356	3123	8.2
Dysprosium	Dy	66	1412	2562	8.6
Holmium	Ho	67	1474	2697	8.8
Erbium	Er	68	1529	2863	9.1
Thulium	Tm	69	1545	1947	9.3
Ytterbium	Yb	70	824	1193	7.0
Lutetium	Lu	71	1656	3395	9.8

The table below contains some information about the properties of some of the actinides. It is difficult to study the remaining eight actinides as they are transuranium **elements** made in tiny amounts.

Element	Symbol	Atomic number	Melting point (°C)	Boiling point (°C)	Density (g/cm³)
Actinium	Ac	89	1047	3197	10.0
Thorium	Th	90	1750	4787	11.7
Protactinium	Pa	91	1840	4027	15.4
Uranium	U	92	1132	3818	18.9
Neptunium	Np	93	640	3902	20.3
Plutonium	Pu	94	641	3232	19.8
Americium	Am	95	994	2607	13.7

Compounds

These tables show you the chemical formulæ of most of the **compounds** mentioned in this book. For example, lanthanum oxide has the formula La_2O_3. This means it is made from two lanthanum **atoms** and three oxygen atoms, joined together by chemical **bonds**.

Lanthanide compounds

Lanthanum compound	Formula
cerium fluoride	CeF_4
cerium nitrate	$Ce(NO_3)_4$
cerium oxide	CeO_2
dysprosium oxide	Dy_2O_3
erbium oxide	Er_2O_3
europium oxide	Eu_2O_3
gadolinium oxide	Gd_2O_3
holmium oxide	Ho_2O_3
lanthanum chloride	$LaCl_3$
lanthanum nitrate	$La(NO_3)_3$
lanthanum oxide	La_2O_3
lutetium oxyorthosilicate	Lu_2SiO_5
neodymium oxide	Nd_2O_3
praseodymium oxide	Pr_2O_3
samarium oxide	Sm_2O_3
terbium oxide	Tb_2O_3
thulium oxide	Tm_2O_3
ytterbium oxide	Yb_2O_3

Find out more continued

Actinide compounds

Actinide compound	Formula
americium chloride	$AmCl_3$
americium oxide	Am_2O_3
berkelium fluoride	$BkCl_3$
curium fluoride	CmF_3
curium oxide	Cm_2O_3
curium(III) chloride	$CmCl_3$
neptunium oxide	NpO_2
plutonium oxide	PuO_2
protactinium iodide	PaI_5
protactinium oxide	Pa_2O_5
sodium diuranate	$Na_2U_2O_7$
thorium nitrate	$Th(NO_3)_4$
thorium oxide	ThO_2
thorium silicate	$ThSiO_4$
uranium ethanoate	$(CH_3COO)_2UO_2$
uranium oxide	U_3O_8
uranium tetrafluoride	UF_4
uranium(IV) oxide	UO_2
uranium(V) oxide	U_2O_5
uranium(VI) oxide	UO_3

Acids

Compound	Formula
hydrochloric acid	HCl
nitric acid	HNO_3
sulphuric acid	H_2SO_4

Other compounds

Other compounds	Formula
calcium chloride	CaF_2
carbon dioxide	CO_2
carbon monoxide	CO
hydrogen fluoride	HF
magnesium fluoride	MgF_2
water	H_2O

Timeline

Element	Year	Discoverer(s)
uranium	1789	Martin Klaproth
cerium	1803	Martin Klaproth; Jöns Berzelius and Wilhlem Hisinger
thorium	1828	Jöns Berzelius
lanthanum	1839	Carl Mosander
erbium	1842	Carl Mosander
terbium	1843	Carl Mosander
holmium	1878	Jacques-Louis Soret and Marc Delafontaine
ytterbium	1878	Jean de Marignac
samarium	1879	Paul-Émile Lecoq
thulium	1879	Per Teodor Cleve
gadolinium	1880	Jean de Marignac
praseodymium	1885	Carl Auer Von Welsbach
neodymium		
dysprosium	1886	Paul-Émile Lecoq
actinium	1899	André Debierne
europium	1901	Eugène Demarçay
lutetium	1907	Carl Auer Von Welsbach and Georges Urbain
protactinium	1913	Kasimir Fajans and Otto Göhring
neptunium	1940	Edwin McMillan and Philip Abelson
plutonium	1940	Glenn Seaborg, Edwin McMillan, Joseph Kennedy and Arthur Wahl
		World's first nuclear reactor starts up
americium	1944	Glenn Seaborg, Ralph James, Leon Morgan and Albert Ghiorso
curium	1944	Glenn Seaborg, Albert Ghiorso and Ralph James
promethium	1945	Jack Marinsky, Lawrence Glendenin, Harold Richter and Charles Coryell
		World's first uranium and plutonium bombs detonated
berkelium	1949	Glenn Seaborg, Stanley Thompson and Albert Ghiorso
californium	1950	Stanley Thompson, Kenneth Street, Albert Ghiorso and Glenn Seaborg
einsteinium	1952	Gregory Choppin, Bernard Harvey, Stanley Thompson and Albert Ghiorso
fermium	1952	Gregory Choppin, Bernard Harvey, Stanley Thompson and Albert Ghiorso
		World's first hydrogen bomb detonated
mendelevium	1955	Gregory Choppin, Bernard Harvey, Stanley Thompson, Albert Ghiorso and Glenn Seaborg
nobelium	1958	Albert Ghiorso, Torbjorn Sikkeland, John Walton & Glenn Seaborg
lawrencium	1961	Albert Ghiorso, Torbjorn Sikkeland, Almon Larsh & Robert Latimer

Glossary

alloy mixture of two or more metals or mixture of a metal and a non-metal. Alloys are often more useful than the pure metal on its own.

alpha radiation (∞ radiation) radiation caused by quickly moving helium nuclei which have broken away from an unstable nucleus

artificial man-made or synthetic

atom smallest particle of an element that has the properties of that element. Atoms contain smaller particles called subatomic particles.

atomic number number of protons in the nucleus of an atom. It is also called the proton number. No two elements have the same atomic number.

base substance that reacts with an acid and neutralizes it. Bases that dissolve in water are also called alkalis.

beta radiation (ß radiation) radiation caused by quickly moving electrons, which have been produced by an unstable nucleus

bond force that joins atoms together

catalyst substance that speeds up reactions without getting used up

ceramic tough solid made by heating clay and other substances to high temperatures in an oven. Plates, bathroom tiles and toilet bowls are made from ceramics.

compound substance made from the atoms of two or more elements, joined together by chemical bonds. Compounds can be broken down into simpler substances and they have different properties from the elements in them. For example, water is a liquid at room temperature, but it is made from two gases, hydrogen and oxygen.

critical mass required amount of a radioactive element for a chain reaction to carry on at a steady rate. On average each atom split causes one more atom to split.

decay break up of the nucleus of a radioactive substance. Radiation is given off and the nucleus of another element is formed.

density mass of a substance compared to its volume. To work out the density of a substance, you divide its mass by its volume. Substances with a high density feel very heavy for their size.

electron subatomic particle with a negative electric charge. Electrons are found around the nucleus of an atom.

element substance made from one type of atom. Elements cannot be broken down into simpler substances. All substances are made from one or more elements.

extract remove a chemical from a mixture of chemicals

gamma radiation (୪ radiation) powerful radiation caused by very high-frequency light waves. Gamma radiation cannot be seen and can pass through metal.

group vertical column of elements in the periodic table. Elements in a group have similar properties.

half-life time taken for half the atoms of a radioactive substance to decay

ion charged particle made when atoms lose or gain electrons. If a metal atom loses electrons it becomes a positive ion. If a non-metal atom gains electrons it becomes a negative ion.

isotope atom of an element with the same number of protons and electrons, but a different number of neutrons, from other isotopes. Isotopes share the same atomic number, but they have different mass numbers.

mass number number of protons and neutrons in the nucleus of an atom, added together

mineral substance that is found naturally, but does not come from animals or plants. Metal ores and limestone are examples of minerals.

molecule smallest unit of an element or compound that exists by itself. A molecule is usually made from two or more atoms joined together.

Glossary continued

neutron subatomic particle with no electric charge. Neutrons are found in the nucleus of an atom.

nuclear reaction reaction involving the nucleus of an atom. Radiation is produced in nuclear reactions.

nucleus part of an atom made from protons and neutrons. It has a positive electric charge and is found at the centre of the atom.

ore mineral from which metals can be taken out and purified

period horizontal row of elements in the periodic table

periodic table table in which all the known elements are arranged into groups and periods

pigment solid substance that gives colour. Pigments do not dissolve in water.

proton subatomic particle with a positive electric charge. Protons are found in the nucleus of an atom.

proton number the number of protons in the nucleus of an atom. It is also called the atomic number. No two elements have the same proton number.

radiation energy or particles given off when an atom decays

radioactive describes a substance that emits energy or particles when an atom decays

reaction chemical change that produces new substances

refining removing impurities from a substance to make it more pure. It can also mean separating the different substances in a mixture, for example, in oil refining.

subatomic particle particle smaller than an atom, such as a proton, neutron or electron

ultraviolet light high-energy light which is invisible to us

weld join between two pieces of metals, usually made by heating them

Further reading and useful websites

Books

Knapp, Brian, *The Elements* series, particularly, *Uranium and Other Radioactive Elements* (Atlantic Europe Publishing Co., 1996)

Oxlade, Chris, *Chemicals in Action* series, particularly, *Elements and Compounds* (Heinemann Library, 2002)

Oxlade, Chris, *Chemicals in Action* series, particularly, *Metals* (Heinemann Library, 2002)

Websites

WebElementsTM
http://www.webelements.com
An interactive periodic table crammed with information and photographs.

Proton Don
http://www.funbrain.com/periodic
The fun periodic table quiz!

Mineralogy Database
http://www.webmineral.com
Lots of useful information about minerals, including colour photographs and information about their chemistry.

DiscoverySchool
http://school.discovery.com/clipart
Help for science projects and homework, and free science clip art.

BBC Science
http://www.bbc.co.uk/science
Quizzes, news, information and games about all areas of science.

Creative Chemistry
http://www.creative-chemistry.org.uk
An interactive chemistry site with fun practical activities, quizzes, puzzles and more.

Index

actinides 7, 32–57
actinium 32, 34–35, 37–38
alloys 9, 11–12, 19, 21, 25,
    28, 36
americium 32, 46, 50–51, 53
Ames process 41
atoms 5, 17, 23, 32, 35, 44,
    46, 56

batteries 12
berkelium 32, 53, 55

californium 32, 54–55, 57
capacitors 26
carbon arc lamps 15
catalysts 15
catalytic converters 15
catalytic cracking 13
cathode ray tubes 22
ceramics 26
cerium 8, 14, 22, 31
cerium oxide 16
chain reactions 44
chemical symbols 35
Chernobyl 45
compounds 4–5
    lanthanide 8–9, 11, 13–16,
    18, 21, 24, 26 28–29, 31
    actinide 34, 36–37, 41–43,
    47, 50, 52, 54
computers 19, 22
control rods 26
critical mass 44, 48
crude oil 13
curium 32, 52
cyclotrons 46, 53, 56–57

depleted uranium 42
deuterons 48
didymia 18
DNA 33
dysprosium 26

earthquakes 30
einsteinium 32, 54–56
electron microscopy 42
electrons 5, 6 17, 23, 46
elements 4–5
enriched uranium 42
erbium 28

europium 22

fermium 32, 55, 57
fibre optic cables 28
fluorescent lamp 22–23, 25

gadolinium 24–25
gas mantles 37
glass 9, 13, 16, 18–19, 21, 28,
    43, 50

half-life 20, 32–33, 38, 49, 53,
    55–57
holmium 27
hydrogen bombs 46, 54–55

ions 23, 46, 48, 52, 54–57
isotopes 20, 29, 32, 38, 42,
    48–49, 54–57

lanthanides 7–31
    isolation of 10–11
lanthanum 4–5, 12
lasers 9, 17, 19, 21, 27, 28–29
lawrencium 32, 57
lenses 13
light 17, 23
lutetium 31

magnetic resonance imaging
    24
magneto-optical disc 24–25
magnets 21
medical imaging 31
medium source rare earth
    lamps 26
mendelevium 32, 56–57
minerals 9,10,18, 21, 36, 40,
    54
    gadolinite 24–25, 28,
    30–31
misch metal 12
missiles 36

neodymium 19
neptunium 32, 47
neutron activation analysis 54
neutrons 5, 26, 29, 32, 34–35,
    44, 48, 52–54
nitrous oxides 15

nobelium 32, 56–57
nuclear fission 44, 46
    fuel 37, 42
    fusion 46
    reactors 26, 42, 45, 47–48,
    55
    weapons 42, 44, 46, 48

periodic table 6, 7, 34, 47, 56
phosphors 9, 22, 25
pigments 19, 43
pitchblende 34, 38, 40
plutonium 32, 48, 55
polystyrene 15
positron emission tomography
    31
praseodymium 18
promethium 9, 20
protactinium 32, 35, 38–39

radiation 31–34, 41, 46
    alpha 33, 40, 48, 50,
    52–53
    beta 20, 33
    gamma 29, 33, 44, 50, 52
radioactive decay 35, 37–39,
    49, 53, 55–57
radioactive waste 49
radioisotope thermoelectric
    generators 49
radiotherapy 33

samarium 20–21, 26
smoke detectors 50–51
space probes 49, 53
stress gauge 30

television sets 16, 19, 25
terbium 25
thorium 32, 35–39
Three Mile Island 45
thulium 29
transuranium elements 47–57
tungsten inert gas welding 36

uranium 32, 35, 38, 39,40–41,
    48

yellow cake 40–41
ytterbium 30

64

Titles in the *Periodic Table* series include:

Hardback   0 431 16995 0

Hardback   0 431 16997 7

Hardback   0 431 16998 5

Hardback   0 431 16996 9

Hardback   0 431 16994 2

Hardback   0 431 16999 3

Find out about the other titles in this series on our website www.heinemann.co.uk/library